All about...

Jacqueline Wilson

Vic Parker

H www.heinemann.co.uk/library

Visit our website to find out more information about **Heinemann Library** books.

To order:
- ☎ Phone 44 (0) 1865 888066
- 🖹 Send a fax to 44 (0) 1865 314091
- 💻 Visit the Heinemann Bookshop at www.heinemann.co.uk/library to browse our catalogue and order online.

First published in Great Britain by Heinemann Library, Halley Court, Jordan Hill, Oxford OX2 8EJ, part of Harcourt Education. Heinemann is a registered trademark of Harcourt Education Ltd.

Editorial: Lucy Thunder and
Helen Cannons
Design: David Poole and Geoff Ward
Picture Research: Rebecca Sodergren
and Kay Altwegg
Production: Edward Moore

Originated by Ambassador Litho Ltd
Printed and bound in Hong Kong, China by
South China Printing

ISBN 0 431 17983 2 (hardback)
07 06 05 04
10 9 8 7 6 5 4 3

ISBN 0 431 17993 X (paperback)
08 07 06 05 04
10 9 8 7 6 5 4 3 2 1

British Library Cataloguing in Publication Data
Parker, Vic
Wilson, Jacqueline. – (All About…)
823.9'14
A full catalogue record for this book is available from the British Library.

Acknowledgements
The Publishers would like to thank the following for permission to reproduce photographs:
Advertising Archive p**17**; Egmont Books Limited p**12**; Hulton Archive p**10**; Hulton Archive/Corbis p**16**; Oxford University Press p**20**; Polka Theatre p**29**; Random House pp**4a**, **4b**, **4c**, **15**, **21**, **22**; Jacqueline Wilson pp**5**, **6**, **7**, **8**, **9**, **11**, **13**, **14**, **18**, **19**, **23**, **24**, **26**, **28**.

Cover photograph of a publicity shot of Jacqueline Wilson, reproduced with permission of Random House.

Sources
The author and Publishers gratefully acknowledge the publications which were used for research and as written sources for this book. Page numbers refer to directly quoted material:
An Interview with Jacqueline Wilson, Joanna Carey (Mammoth, 2000)
The *Guardian* website –
http://books.guardian.co.uk pp. **22, 23** Stories from the Web –
www.storiesfromtheweb.org pp. **20, 21, 28, 29**
Transworld Books website –
www.kidsatrandomhouse.co.uk/jacquelinewilson/
p. **4**
Fiction works by Jacqueline Wilson are cited in the text.

The Publishers would like to thank Stephen Noon for his assistance in the preparation of this book.

Contents

Any words shown in the text in bold, **like this**, are
explained in the Glossary.

The author and Publishers would like to thank Jacqueline
Wilson for her invaluable help in the writing of this book.

Who is Jacqueline Wilson?

Jacqueline Wilson is one of the most popular story-tellers writing for young people today. She is famous all over the world for books such as *The Story of Tracy Beaker*, *The Bed and Breakfast Star*, *Double Act* and *The Illustrated Mum*, among many others. Over ten million copies of her books have been sold in the UK alone.

Writing about real life

Jacqueline has said: 'The tradition in children's books used to be that there was a beginning, a middle and an ending, and the ending was the happy bit. Now, real life isn't like that for most children.' Her stories are about kids with problems familiar to many young people today, such as being bullied or fitting into a step-family. Boys and especially girls everywhere love reading about her true-to-life **characters**. Jacqueline's books have won several major awards and have been turned into highly popular TV programmes and plays.

▲ Some of Jacqueline's famous books.

What does Jacqueline look like?

Jacqueline is a familiar figure to many of her readers because she spends lots of time visting schools, libraries and bookshops to meet them. She describes herself as 'small and skinny with very short spiky hair and silver glasses. I nearly always wear black and I have a big silver ring on every finger.'

▲ The face behind the stories.

Factfile

★ Date of birth	17 December 1945
★ Star sign	Sagittarius
★ Eye colour	Greeny-brown
★ Hair colour	Used to be brown, now silver
★ Pets	None
★ Hobbies	Swimming, reading, line dancing, visiting art galleries, watching films
★ Favourite food	Fruit and cakes
★ Favourite book	Different ones at different times! At the moment, *Adventures With Rosalind* by Charlotte Austen, which has long been out of print.
★ Bad habits	Being very untidy
★ Personal motto	'Give it a go!'

Early years

Jacqueline Aitken (she became Wilson when she got married) was born in the city of Bath, in England, on 17 December 1945. This was just after the end of World War II – a terrible war that had been going on for six years. Many thousands of people died, either through joining the fighting or being bombed at home.

People who fell in love in wartime often got married quickly, because they did not know what might happen in the future. Jacqueline's parents met at a dance in a famous old building in Bath called the Pump Room. Her mother was doing office work for the **navy**. Her father was a draughtsman, a job which involved drawing skilful plans of machinery and buildings. It was not long before the couple got married and they wasted no time in having a baby. Jacqueline was born just a year later.

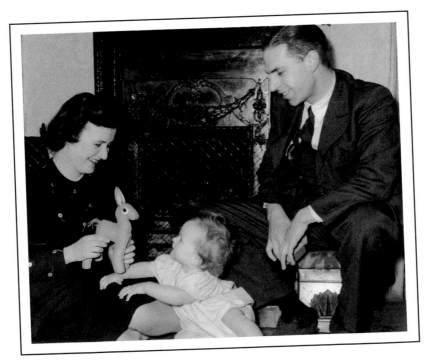

▲ Baby Jacqueline with her mother and father in 1946.

Living with Grandma and Grandpa

When Jacqueline was about three years old, her father changed job and took the family to live in Kingston upon Thames, near London. For a while they shared a house with Jacqueline's grandparents, who lived downstairs.

Jacqueline liked playing with her grandma very much. Her grandma had been a hat-maker, so she was excellent at sewing. She made wonderful outfits for all of Jacqueline's dolls, with special clothes like nightdresses and winter coats.

Jacqueline with her grandparents. ▶

Ideas from real life

Jacqueline's main character in *The Lottie Project*, an eleven-year-old girl called Charlie, also once lived in her grandparents' house. Unlike Jacqueline, Charlie did not enjoy it much. Charlie describes what it was like for herself and her mother, Jo:

'Jo and I haven't always had a home. We lived with Grandma and Grandpa at first. That was pretty bad. Grandma is the sort of lady who keeps a damp flannel neatly folded in a plastic bag and she's forever whipping it out and smearing round imaginary sticky bits.'

Going to school

Jacqueline and her mother and father soon moved into a **council flat** and Jacqueline started school. She had a difficult time at first because she fell ill with one nasty illness after another, such as measles and whooping cough. She was so ill that she had to have several months off school. When Jacqueline was well enough to go back, she found that everyone had already made friends. Fitting in was hard. However, when she was six she moved to a school called Latchmere Primary and soon settled in. Jacqueline loved English, Art, country dancing, and Friday afternoons, which was when the teacher read a story out loud. She also remembers crying over school dinners, which she thought were horrible!

Jacqueline in her Latchmere Primary School uniform.

At breaktimes, Jacqueline liked to make up and act out vivid imaginary games. They were so detailed that many of her friends found them too strange and could not join in properly:

'We used to play a game where we climbed a very tall tree to get up to a treehouse. Many years later when I took my daughter to that school, I looked for the tree. I couldn't find it anywhere. It had been one of my imaginary games – but in my memory it was so real!'

The secret room

One year, Jacqueline was chosen to be Christmas card monitor. This meant she was in charge of the pupils' Christmas cards. Her teacher showed her where to take the cards for safe-keeping. In the school hall there were some hidden stairs, and at the top was a store room no one else knew about. The store room was piled high with magical costumes from different school plays.

Jacqueline shared her exciting secret with a small group of friends. At lunchtimes, as often as they dared, they crept away to try on the wonderful costumes and pretend they were different characters.

Jacqueline (right) and a school friend with her favourite teacher, Mr Townsend. ▶

Bad hair days

Like many girls, Jacqueline wanted to have beautiful long hair like the princesses in stories. One of Jacqueline's closest friends, Ann, had long wavy hair just like she longed for. Unfortunately for Jacqueline, her own hair was straight and fine. To make things worse, her mother wanted her to have short, curly hair like the child movie star Shirley Temple. So she made Jacqueline have a cut and **perm** regularly. The perms made Jacqueline's hair go into a tight, frizzy mass, which she hated!

Jacqueline's mother loved the child movie star Shirley Temple, with her mop of curls.

Feeling different

At school, Jacqueline was teased for having short, frizzy hair. Another girl, Pat, was made fun of for being overweight. One of Jacqueline's closest friends, Christine, went through an extremely difficult time when her mother died. Today, Jacqueline's stories often focus on kids in difficult circumstances like these.

Growing up

Jacqueline grew up without any brothers or sisters. However, she enjoyed being on her own and did not feel lonely. Jacqueline liked walking to school by herself, because she could make up stories in her head without anyone interrupting. After school, Jacqueline was always home alone for a while before her mother came back from the cake shop where she worked. This gave her time to play the endless imaginary games she loved.

Treasured toys

When Jacqueline was about eight, she longed to have a dog. However, pets were not allowed in **council flats**. Jacqueline's mother bought her a very realistic little black toy dog instead. She also helped Jacqueline to collect many interesting dolls. Jacqueline loved to think about what each doll would be like if it could walk and talk.

Jacqueline with three of the dolls in her collection. ▶

Beloved books

Jacqueline adored reading. When she was very young, her father read aloud her favourite stories, like Enid Blyton's *The Magic Faraway Tree*. Later, on her own, she read to herself for hours and hours at a time. Jacqueline made countless trips to the library to borrow popular stories, like *The Family from One End Street* by Eve Garnett. She found it very frustrating when the books she wanted to borrow were not in. She had to read all the Mary Poppins books in the wrong order! Jacqueline thought the best thing was to actually own books, so you could read them whenever you wanted. Every birthday and summer holiday she was given a new book for her collection.

This was one of Jacqueline's first favourite books.

Days out

Jacqueline's parents argued a lot, so they did not do many things together. However, Jacqueline's dad sometimes took her into the countryside for a day out walking. Once, Jacqueline's mum found out where the offices of the big movie companies were in London. She took Jacqueline there so she could ask for pictures of her favourite film star, Mandy Miller.

▲ Jacqueline on a day out with her mum and dad.

Writing her own stories

Jacqueline was not content with reading other people's stories. From the age of seven or eight, she spent lots of time making up her own, too. She copied out drawings into a blank notebook, then invented stories to go with her pictures. Sometimes Jacqueline looked in sewing pattern books for people to cut out and stick down. She used these fashion models as **characters** in her stories, too!

At secondary school

When Jacqueline was eleven, she went to a brand new girls' secondary school in New Malden called Coombe School. She passed an exam called the **eleven plus**, so she was put in classes for the brightest pupils. Jacqueline was excellent at English, although the teacher thought she wrote too much **slang**! She was also good at Art and History. However, she was hopeless at any subject involving numbers, such as Maths and Science. Jacqueline also hated Games, because she could not catch or hit a ball.

Exam time

At the age of sixteen, Jacqueline took her **O levels**. She thought that she would do very well in some subjects, but very badly in others, no matter how hard she tried. So in the evenings before

▲ Jacqueline (left) and a friend in their Coombe School uniforms.

the exams, Jacqueline did not bother to stay in and **revise**. Instead, she went out with her boyfriend. When she took her exams, she was very unprepared.

Jacqueline left school with five or six O levels. She was fed up with strict, stuffy school life and being told what to do. She would have liked to continue studying English, but nobody explained that she could go on to a college. Jacqueline wondered whatever to do next.

▲ Similar to Jacqueline, Tim, in her book *Cliffhanger*, hates games. Then he has to face an action-packed adventure holiday…

What Jacqueline says

Jacqueline knew from a very early age that she wanted to be a writer:

'As a teenager, I put all the effort that I should have put into homework into writing. I wrote a full-length **novel** at the age of fifteen. I longed to get a book **published**, but I was from the sort of background where people just didn't become writers. My ambition seemed like a shiny dream that would never come true…'

Becoming a writer

When Jacqueline left school in 1961, there were not as many job choices for girls as there are now. Most girls became shop assistants, secretaries, nurses or teachers. Jacqueline's parents encouraged her to do a secretarial course, and after nearly a year she began looking for a job. One day, a newspaper advert caught her eye – but it was not for a secretary. A magazine company was looking for teenage writers.

Jacqueline sent in one of the many stories she had written. It was a funny tale about a girl who went to a disco, but was not asked to dance by any of the boys. The company liked it and bought it! Jacqueline was amazed and thrilled. The feeling of earning money for writing was wonderful. Even better, the company bought several more of her stories and then offered her a job!

▲ After leaving school in 1961, Jacqueline went to a secretarial school, like this one.

A writer at last!

Jacqueline left home and went to live in Dundee, Scotland, where the magazine company had its office. It was a brave thing to do, because she was still only seventeen and she knew no one at all in Scotland.

The magazine company printed very popular comics for boys and magazines for women. Jacqueline did all sorts of writing for the women's magazines, such as the star signs and the readers' letters. She was told to make them all up!

Every Christmas a *Jackie* annual came out with new material and the best bits from the previous year.

A famous name

Every Friday afternoon, Jacqueline had to report to the two people who had offered her a job: Mr Cuthbert and Mr Tate. They thought that for someone so young, she was an extremely promising writer. When they launched a new magazine for teenage girls, they named it after her! Jacqueline was 'Jackie' to all her friends, so that is what they called the magazine. It became the best selling magazine for teenage girls. Jacqueline sometimes wrote for it, too.

Life in Dundee

In Dundee, Jacqueline lived in a Church of Scotland **hostel** with other girls of a similar age. It was rather like a boarding school. Most of the girls went home at weekends, but Jacqueline lived too far away to do this and was left there feeling **homesick**. Then Jacqueline started seeing a boyfriend called Millar Wilson, whose mother invited her for tasty dinners on Saturdays and Sundays. Jacqueline and Millar fell in love. In 1965, when Jacqueline was nineteen, they got married.

▲ Here are the girls that shared the Church of Scotland hostel with Jacqueline. She is standing in the back row at the far right.

Breaking into books

The couple moved back to Jacqueline's home town of Kingston upon Thames, where Millar joined the police force. Alone at home all day, Jacqueline wrote all the time. She still sold her writing to magazines, but what she really wanted to have **published** was a **novel**. She worked on several novels – all for adults. However, to Jacqueline's disappointment, book **publishers** turned them down.

▲ Jacqueline as a young mum with her daughter, Emma.

In 1967, Jacqueline and Millar had a daughter, Emma. Jacqueline loved being a mum, but she still worked hard at her writing, too. She even wrote some funny magazine articles on coping with a baby! Jacqueline enjoyed hunting out good stories to read to Emma. Emma was about two when Jacqueline came across a series of children's books called *Nippers*. She tried writing a story for the series and sent it to the publisher. To her delight, it became her first published book: *Ricky's Birthday*.

A burning ambition

Jacqueline was disappointed to find that the next story she wrote for the *Nippers* series was turned down. She had better luck writing for grown-ups and had five adult crime novels published. However, Jacqueline knew in her heart of hearts that she wanted to write for children. Some authors write stories about children, but Jacqueline wanted to write stories from the child's own point of view.

A children's author

Jacqueline wrote her first children's novel in the late 1970s. It was a story for teenagers, called *Nobody's Perfect*. At first it was rejected by several publishers, but it was finally accepted by Oxford University Press. Jacqueline was spurred on to write several more teenage books. All her stories focused on girls of around fifteen years old. Then her **editor** moved to another company. He suggested that Jacqueline might like to write books for a younger age group for this publisher. They had no idea that this change of writing style would bring Jacqueline fame and fortune...

The original 1982 cover for Jacqueline's first published teenage book.

A new style

Jacqueline already had ideas in her head for a younger story about a child **in care** who wanted to be **fostered**. She asked for black-and-white line drawings to go with the story, like the illustrations she had loved in her own childhood books. Jacqueline's editor suggested an artist called Nick Sharratt, who Jacqueline thought was wonderful. She loved the way Nick used his pictures to help tell her story. When *The Story of Tracy Beaker* was finally published in 1991, it was a huge success. It was **shortlisted** for two top awards – the Smarties Prize and the Carnegie Medal.

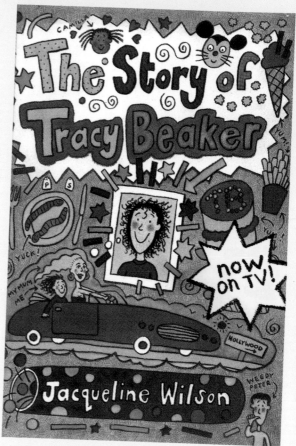

▲ This story really made Jacqueline's name as a writer.

What the readers say

The Story of *Tracy Beaker* remains one of Jacqueline's best-loved books:

'Most of my mates have read this book and they all loved it. I would say it is very real and moving, so be prepared to laugh and cry. Once you start reading, you can't stop.'

(Jill, age 12, from Peterborough, UK)

'It was brilliant. I really like it because I am in care and it is nice to know someone knows how we all feel inside.'

(Joanne, age 12, from Chesterfield, UK)

The successful author

Since *The Story of Tracy Beaker*, Jacqueline has had around 40 books for children **published**. Some much-loved, fun stories are for very young children. These include *The Werepuppy, Freddy's Teddy, Mark Spark in the Dark, The Dinosaur's Packed Lunch, My Brother Bernadette* and *The Monster Story-teller*. Yet it is stories for readers aged from seven or eight and over for which Jacqueline has become most famous, all over the world.

Some of her most popular for this age are *The Suitcase Kid, The Bed and Breakfast Star, Double Act, Sleepovers, The Mum-minder, Dustbin Baby, Take a Good Look, The Lottie Project*, the *Girls…* series and *The Illustrated Mum*.

This picture from *The Illustrated Mum* shows Nick Sharratt's simple, but effective, drawing style.

The secret of Jacqueline's success

Jacqueline's work is so popular because she writes very realistically from a child's point of view. She tackles difficult situations that are at the centre of thousands of readers' lives, such as **divorce**, **poverty** and **mental illness**, and she writes about these complicated issues with understanding and humour. Jacqueline's perfect partnership with Nick Sharratt has also been magical!

Jacqueline with illustrator Nick Sharratt – a truly talented pair. ▶

A typical day

Jacqueline lives by herself in a small terraced house in Kingston upon Thames. (She and Millar separated several years ago.) Early every morning, Jacqueline starts the day by swimming 50 lengths of her local pool. She is not really an early-morning sort of person, but she forces herself to do it. It is good exercise, and it also gives her time to think. By the time Jacqueline gets back, she is feeling great. She then has breakfast and opens her post. She receives over 200 readers' letters every week!

Some days, Jacqueline then sits down to write. However, as a world-famous author, there are lots of things she has to do besides making up great stories. There are many days when Jacqueline has to go out to a school visit or to give a bookshop talk or to a meeting to discuss the business side of her work. She likes to travel to places on the train, so she can work during the journey.

◀ Jacqueline in her living room.

Writing on the move

Jacqueline can get into her writing very quickly. This is because when Emma was little, Jacqueline could only write in the short periods while her daughter was at nursery or having a daytime nap. So, she trained her brain to get down to work fast! The train journey from Jacqueline's house to London takes about half an hour. In that half an hour, she can jot down 500 words or more in a notebook! Then she'll manage another 500 words or so on the way back…

Jacqueline's daughter Emma is now grown up. She lives about three hours' drive away in Cambridge, where she teaches French at a college and writes books for students. At six o'clock each evening, Jacqueline phones Emma for a chat. They natter for about half an hour – or more! Jacqueline and Emma are best friends. Besides speaking every day on the phone, they send each other a postcard every day, too. They sometimes go on holiday together, and Jacqueline says that these are her very best times of all.

After supper, Jacqueline sometimes goes out line dancing or to a pub quiz or to the theatre or cinema with a friend. Other times she stays in and watches TV while replying to her readers' letters. She tries her best to write back to everyone, but it is impossible! At around ten o'clock she stops working and reads for an hour or two before bed.

How Jacqueline works

Jacqueline has a work desk upstairs, but she can write anywhere. She writes using pen and paper because she has always liked to buy pretty exercise books and fancy pens, ever since she was a child. Later, she types everything up on a laptop computer. She can not move it around because it is wired up to different bits of equipment and she does not know how to unplug everything and link it all back together!

Jacqueline Wilson on Jacqueline Wilson

Here are some of Jacqueline's answers to questions we asked her:

What is your house like?
'Small and shabby, and crammed with lots and lots of books (over 10,000 at the last count!). I have heaps of pictures everywhere, from framed Nick Sharratt artwork to odd little postcards, and lots of strange stuff like a full-sized fashion model who lives in my bedroom.'

Why do you wear so much silver jewellery?
'I read that the author E. Nesbit bought a new bangle whenever she had a new book **published**. I liked the idea, so I do the same. I wear lots of rings because people did that in the 1970s and the habit stuck. I hope I don't still wear anything else from the 1970s!'

▲ Jacqueline and Nick Sharratt receiving a Smarties Prize in 2000 for *Lizzie Zipmouth*.

Where do you get your ideas from?
'I don't just decide to write about some problem or other. I get ideas from making up an imaginary **character** and finding out about their life.'

What would you be if you weren't a writer?
'When I was a child, I loved brushing other people's long hair, so I wanted to be a hairdresser. But I think I would have made a much better bookseller than a hairdresser.'

What is the best thing about being a writer?
'You don't just live one life, you live lots of different lives inside your head.'

What is the worst thing about being a writer?
'The fear that I might wake up one morning and not be able to do it any more. Also, you never feel at peace because you've always got ideas leaping around inside your head!'

When are you going to stop writing?
'Stopping writing would be like stopping cleaning my teeth!'

If you would like to stay in touch with all the latest news about Jacqueline Wilson and her books, you can join the official Jacqueline Wilson fanclub at

www.randomhouse.co.uk/childrens/jacquelinewilson/fanclub/home.htm.

Jacqueline today

Jacqueline has said that one of the best things about her job is meeting lots and lots of children. She visits schools or libraries or bookshops to talk to her readers an average of three times a week. She has also travelled in Europe, the USA and Australia on book tours. Jacqueline sometimes gets ideas for **characters** from the children she meets at these events! Jacqueline has no major ambitions for the future. She is pleased with all she has achieved and very content in her home life and her work. Jacqueline has had offers from **publishers** to write other types of books, such as more novels for grown-ups, but she has turned them down. She wants to stick with the children's stories she loves writing best!

How to write like Jacqueline

Jacqueline's fans always ask her what they should do to become a writer. Her advice is to read lots and keep a diary as a simple way to get used to writing each day. Most of all, enjoy your writing!

Jacqueline regularly meets her fans at signings like this.

A passion for writing

Jacqueline is delighted that some of her books have been turned into plays at the theatre or programmes on TV. She even played a small part in the TV version of *Double Act*!

Today, Jacqueline is kept very busy with invitations to talk about her work and she writes every day, no matter where she is or what else she has to do. She has plenty of ideas for many more stories!

▲ The programme for the Polka Theatre production of *The Lottie Project*.

What the readers say

Jacqueline Wilson has fans all over the world:

'The Illustrated Mum *is one of the best books I've ever read...*
Jacqueline Wilson *is someone who I would love to write like.*'
　　　　(Zareen, age 8, from Spilsby, UK)

'I thought Girls Under Pressure *was a wonderful book because many
girls can relate to Ellie and her friends, Nadine and Magda.*'
　　　　(Cate, age 12, from Boston, USA)

'Most of my friends love Jacqueline Wilson.'
　　　　(Laura, age 11, from New Zealand)

Timeline

1945 Jacqueline is born
1962 First story is **published**
1962 Goes to work for a magazine publisher in Glasgow
1965 Marries Millar
1967 Their daughter, Emma, is born
1969 First storybook is published – *Ricky's Birthday*
1982 First novel for older children published – *Nobody's Perfect*
1991 First book illustrated by Nick Sharratt – *The Story of Tracy Beaker*
1993 *The Suitcase Kid* wins the Children's Book Award
2000 *The Illustrated Mum* wins NIBBY and *Guardian* awards
2002 Jacqueline gains the OBE, an award given by the Queen

Books by Jacqueline Wilson

Here are some books by Jacqueline you might like to read:

The Suitcase Kid (first published in 1993)
Andy's parents **divorce** and she finds she has to split her time between two new families...

The Lottie Project (first published in 1997)
Charlie begins a history project which turns out not to be as boring as she expects when she discovers a Victorian girl who was her double...

The Illustrated Mum (first published in 1999)
Marigold is not like other mothers. She has tattoos for a start. How will her daughters, Dolphin and Star, cope with her unusual behaviour?

Glossary

characters people in a story

council flat rented flat owned by the government department that runs a town or city

divorce when a couple end their marriage

editor person in a publishing company whose job is to work with an author to make their story as good as possible

eleven plus exam that children used to take at age eleven to decide which secondary school they would go to. Only a few places still do this.

foster when foster parents sign an official agreement to look after a child for a while

homesick feeling upset because you miss your home and family

hostel a place where young people can stay

in care when children are looked after in a children's home, rather than by their parents or foster parents

mental illness illness that affects thoughts and feelings

navy military organization in charge of boats and submarines

novel book-length story

O levels exams that used to be taken at age sixteen, before GCSEs were introduced

perm type of hair treatment that makes straight hair go curly for several months

poverty not having very much money and having to go without things you need

publish when a publisher turns a story into a book for sale

publisher person or company that makes and sell books

reviewer person who writes a review (their opinion) about a new book, film, music or art exhibition

revise to go over school work and try to remember it for an exam

shortlist stage before the final choice in a competition. Being shortlisted is the next best thing to winning a competition.

slang informal words that people use, like 'OK' and 'Cool!'

Index

Titles in the *All About Authors* series are:

Hardback　　0 431 17982 4

Hardback　　0 431 17986 7

Hardback　　0 431 17981 6

Hardback　　0 431 17987 5

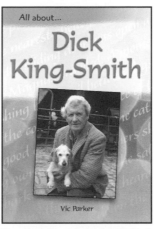

Hardback　　0 431 17988 3

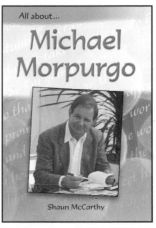

Hardback　　0 431 17985 9

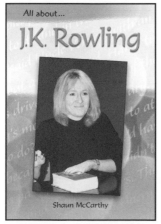

Hardback　　0 431 17980 8

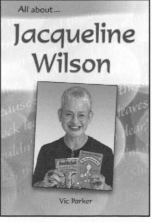

Hardback　　0 431 17983 2

Find out about the other titles in this series on our website www.heinemann.co.uk/library